NEVERTHELESS

NEVER THE LESS

WALKING POEMS

GILLIAN JEROME

NIGHTWOOD EDITIONS

2022

Nightwood Editions
P.O. Box 1779
Gibsons, BC VON 1VO
Canada
www.nightwoodeditions.com

COVER DESIGN: Angela Yen
TYPOGRAPHY: Carleton Wilson

Nightwood Editions acknowledges the support of the Canada Council for the Arts, the
Government of Canada, and the Province of British Columbia through the BC Arts Council.

This book has been produced on 100% post-consumer recycled, ancient-forest-free paper,
processed chlorine-free and printed with vegetable-based dyes.

Printed and bound in Canada.

LIBRARY AND ARCHIVES CANADA CATALOGUING IN PUBLICATION

Title: Nevertheless : walking poems / Gillian Jerome.
Names: Jerome, Gillian, 1974- author.
Identifiers: Canadiana (print) 20220151342 | Canadiana (ebook) 20220151369 |
    ISBN 9780889714120 (softcover) | ISBN 9780889714137 (EPUB)
Subjects: LCGFT: Poetry.
Classification: LCC PS8619.E76 N48 2022 | DDC C811/.6—dc23

For Roro and Micah, and for Laura—

Il a dit
Marcher vers le soleil
Marcher
—Richard Baillargeon, *Champs / La Mer, triptyque 1*

But in its premodern expressions, mapmaking was a pursuit that mingled knowledge and supposition, that told stories about places, that admitted fear, love, memory and amazement into its projections.
—Robert MacFarlane, *The Wild Places*

Contents

Reveries of a Walker Walking Among Others

Personals (Odes)

Desire Lines

REVERIES OF A WALKER WALKING AMONG OTHERS

I am making my way in some dark room
looking for other structures to love.
—Peter Gizzi, "When Orbital Proximity Feels Creepy"

Reveries of a Walker Walking Among Others

> You have to be very keen and very alert to recognize the new
> manifestations of just one person.
> —Thich Nhat Hanh, *No Death, No Fear*

At night I count
    not the stars
but the freckles
    on your head—

    *

When I walk to the sea,
    the tide rolling out
& in
    is a feeling—

    *

    I see the sea of them:
on your forehead, face, elbows, arms, you
    asleep on your hospice bed
your hair a white

    bolt of lightning
childhood storms
    cracking me open—

    *

As for the feeling,
         that everything is
always moving—

         coming
                  going—

         *

         You asleep:
the body
         I climbed onto
& claimed—

         *

Sleep's a sea
         I want to be set
free in—

         *

"When you died

         it was like
a whole
         library burned down—"

         *

         You: tiny, bobbing
black arrow pointing
         this way & that—

utterly
         inconspicuous.

*

When you left
       the shape we took up
grew.

*

I see you in
       our feet—

*

I hear you in
       the crows' abrupt
trades
       of code.

*

At night I leave
       the house
with a leash & keys—

the dog meanders
       alongside me.
We stop & stand

       at the edge of the trees, squint
inside the blackness lit
       up by the moon

& listen for you.

Atmosphere

Am listening to the light rain.
Am listening to the cold wind.
      It says *keep*
moving. Here we are in
      the Arbutus corridor
walking—

     *

     Standing at the edge of a shimmering copper puddle
behind the Molson Brewery by the Burrard Street Bridge
     under which a woman in a black hoodie
with her Lab lives in her truck,
     black-capped chickadees
sing about how to care
     for everything *tenderly*
even the plastic Double Gulp cup
     from 7-Eleven, even
the four castaway milk jugs—

     *

Thank you, dear chickadees
Thank you, benevolent sparrows
Thank you, wild raspberries
Thank you birch trees & all of your hundreds
of golden rotting leaves
Thank you, dear readers,
for showing up—

     *

Am following the eleven-kilometre line built by CPR
        trying to see how we did this:
a study in occupation in possibilities
        for human connection
but also a study in movement—

        *

        Inside the blackberry bushes
a man with black hair and dark eyes sleeps inside a plastic cylinder
        kept dry by a blue tarp—

        *

"There you are. Here is
        your cheque with your name on it
for $11,250. Take it. If
        you do not, you will never
get a cent for your reserve."

        *

        "The fish swam there, taking a
breather from their ocean playgrounds, ducks
        gathered, women cultivated camas fields & berries
abounded. On the sandbar,
        Musqueam, Tsleil-Waututh and Squamish women
till oyster and clam beds to
        encourage reproduction."

        *

By 1914, each remaining Skwxwú7mesh person
        living here at Snauq was paid $11,250
to make way for a gravel company,
        for a fancy resto called the Sandbar

where one can pay $17 for a bamboo steamer basket filled with
    shrimp & pork dumplings.

        *

        A century later, the Sḵwx̱wú7mesh Nation
placed this welcome pole
        across from the fishing boats at False Creek—
Today a mallard duck takes
        flight in the totem, a whale's tale
emerges from the water, from the wood.
        A raven, at the heart of the wood, watches.

        *

"Once a monk asked Changsha,
        Zen Master Jingcen,
'How do you turn mountains, rivers,
        and great earth into the self?'
Changsha said, 'How do you turn the self
        into mountains, rivers and great earth?'"

        *

Look at you zooming by
        on your moped. Look at you in your white cap
puttering along pushing your walker—
        And you pushing your brother
in his wheelchair—
        And you mother & daughter
laughing your guts out—
        And you middle-aged couple
holding hands—

*

Look at you, old hose.
And you, shopping cart filled with old bicycle parts
       & mouldy clothes—
Thank you for showing up.

*

"There needs to be less tourism," said the guy
       on the bicycle to his friend. "And
there needs to be more—" Dunno. The wind
       took him.

*

With his arms held out to you,
       inviting you—

The Messenger

My name comes to me like an angel.

—Tomas Tranströmer, "The Name"

Your name comes to me like morning light wavering on the water

Like a plate of butter biscuits like butter

Like a bicycle in flight

Your name comes to me like the fuchsia shirt & shimmering
    copper pants

you put on after we woke up this morning before sunrise

& danced in your living room

& all the dreams of my childhood came back to me

Like the ravine we grew up in like the creek water that ran through it

Like rivulets popping out of rock

Like clay bursting open

The earth gives us so much:

This morning's foggy walk through X̱wáýx̱way under cedars

The ocean water we dip our hands into

The salt on my fingers

The flock of Barrow's goldeneye ducks who

flew together just above the water at Third Beach this morning

flying like dancers in unison

The coyote who appears before us who is part wolf

He looks at us like family

He looks out for us like family

At night, after we fall to sleep together

we come here like dancers

like wolves who are part coyote

In our dreams we clean up the microplastics

In our dreams we restore the reindeer

We travel north in solidarity

In our dreams the brown bodies the black bodies

the children in prison here and yonder go free—

In our dreams the ebullient silver bodies come back as salmon

The coral is beautiful again

In our dreams not all the birds return but

our home is the aviary is the apiary is the open sky—

Your name comes to me like the birch tree I climbed each day
    of my childhood

Like all the daytime reveries I was punished for

Reveries so delicious now that we're free

When the children come they come as clowns

They come as pirates their booty is butterflies

They ride their ponies They wear crowns of peonies—

Your name comes to me like my father's

gentleness speaking to us from the cedars

Like a black oystercatcher eating a limpet

Like a black oystercatcher whose red luminous beak

calls to us this morning against this backdrop of grey

Like a glass-bottomed boat

Like a pod of orcas swimming in the seas that need healing

Your name comes to me like an utterance

Like a half-conscious trip to the toilet in the middle of the night

Like the textures proffered by your testicles in my hand—

In another life we rode a starship together we rode a steamship
    I wore a bonnet, briefly—

We eschewed the gold rush & the gold

In my dream you poured ambrosia over my head with a ladle

& I lasted

What I thought was wrong with me was not wrong

What you thought was wrong with you wasn't wrong

Will you try to stay open to me like an egg?

You know of my body's coldness you know my thin blood

Sometimes in our sleep you wrap my body in your body

Sometimes your heart's a wavelength, the only arrhythmia of
    the night—

Sometimes I dream you are catching a fish to feed us

Sometimes I feel the fire that belongs to us all

At night I dream you are braiding my hair

& the wolves come to keep us company

& their breath smells like fire like honey

Between my green eyes between your green eyes

so much moving in unison so much laughter

& fumbling & endless coconut butter—

Your name comes to me like the sound of pirate children playing
    in the boat

Like the first light of my girls like their pink faces like the vernix
    they wore like coats

Like the silence we swim in that sounds like love.

Often I'm Permitted to Return to These Cedars

The curled boughs of these cedars
        carry me
their rough trunks
        split into a tuning fork—

whose big sweet noise lands
        me on the path
with all of my edginess intact.

        Raindrops spring in & out of the puddles
BMW SUV barrels past the Max 30 km/h sign
        Every living thing finding its frequency:

the guy in the burgundy smoking jacket
        the labourer who hammers asbestos walls until
they pop out, fly down two floors below

        where they smash into rubble.
Even the snail who has come so fully out
        of its spiral shell like a fat tongue

gliding in its own saliva, eyes cocked out
        from its tentacles,
angles toward the middle of the path, alone

        but not thrown by it.

Walking One Spring Evening at Trimble Park

A woman with a grey mullet sits on the bench across from St. Helen's Anglican Church at Trimble & 8th barefoot, cradling her swollen left foot & its yellowed toenails. Bright red poppies and purple irises shoot up around her. Says she knows everybody, sits here in the evenings— back at home, she doesn't talk to anybody all day except her two cats, Oscar and Juno. Her husband is a bricklayer, her kids work construction. Back in Russia, she says, people talk to each other all the time on the street, in the grocery store lineup. "Here, every man is an island." She calls out across the street, to the white-haired man walking his poodles, "Hello Tom"—that's my yoga teacher, she says—"Will you marry me?" She smiles minus a front tooth and says, "You say yes to me out of pity."

"Pity," says Tom, "is never the best response. Besides, I'm still married." When she laughs, her wide, ruddy face lights up. The smell of cherry blossoms sugars the air—summer is coming to Vancouver. "Soon," she says, "we'll go down to Jericho, buy smokies & watch the seals."

Poem for Fraser Street

Outside Yummy Fat's Kitchen,
     a man with tattoos up his arms
walks two Shih Tzus on red leashes.

     Mothers count coupons

in the entrance to No Frills.
     Pensioners line up
for Bingo Night at the Elks Lodge.

     Outside Fred's Automotive
a washed-up silver fox steps into
     his Chevrolet Chevelle.

Three women sit at the bus stop bench
     with umpteen bags from Save-On-Foods
their swollen feet hanging out their sandals.

     Meanwhile, the Testigos de Jehová pass out pamphlets
in front of the Dollar Tree.
     The construction worker in the Carhartts laughs

& hands the pamphlet back
     to the woman in florals.
Over yonder a man asleep

     on the sidewalk holds a half-eaten pork
bun in his hand.

Walking in Strathcona

Right in front of the Georgia Viaduct
            on Union Street four Black women
walk toward me laughing & I think of Hogan's Alley

        a whole community razed
to the ground for this ugly, soon-to-be-
            dismantled viaduct.

Demolition, the trope of this city's
            history. I sit myself down
at the Wilder Snail where

        bluegrass plays. People writing,
people working, people talking about work.
        Sign says *Restrooms for Consumers*

only. Tampons 99 cents. Here you can buy
        Avalon milk by the bottle.
Plus a guide to being a Green Mama.

        At the park, a man talks to himself.
A woman lays herself down in the grass.
        Kids run through the sprinklers

dump buckets of water on each other.
        A man sharing the bench with me smokes a joint.
A woman chews on a chicken wing.

        Further on, a boy carries his cat
half the size of his body
        homeward—

Neighbourhood Poem

The sun is thick in its business of setting
We throw a ball out on the front lawn

after burgers, homemade fries, freestyling
notes on the piano—

Try not to bean each other by
eyeing the ball mid-arc & catching it

without stomping on the lavender.
You're ten, tall, gap-toothed, shoulders

burnt by the sun—you laugh when you catch
the ball, crack your gum

Ask if we can stop playing, go
somewhere, go for a walk

around the neighbourhood.
We find & name the neighbour's

heather, hibiscus, rhododendrons.
When you spot the Block Watch sign

you ask me, *Why do people
need a reason to look out for each other?*

PERSONALS (ODES)

Poem for Laura

We each married a poet
& each by each we

left them. My friend Mary said
it's hard to love a big shot even

harder to leave a big shot—
but we did.

Nights we sit up,
me grading papers in Vancouver,

you in Toronto watching *RuPaul's Drag Race*,
both of us eating chips from the bag,

cackling till our guts
hurt. We eat late. Read late. Feel

4,382 kilometres closer than the last
time we caught up. Crows hide their tiniest

trinkets in our hair. Days unfurl their bright
moments: good salads, a seat on the bus, nary

a meeting runneth over—
After work, we take our kids out
to Chinatown for dumplings.

Wash out the glass containers from lunch.
Me talking you talking late

about whatever's whirling around
in our systems. What it feels like to

inhale a new lover. Bit by awesome
bit the old stories fade

away—we keep travelling
through the days together

swapping what we've been reading,
podcasts, plans for work, worries

re lawyers, re kids. Stitching new
silvery linings through our lives.

In your house by the train tracks, wheels
turn, you struggle to sleep so

I sprinkle some fairy dust on
your blackish nightie and say "Night, L.

Talk mañana." Sometimes it takes years
for myths to implode. Soon we grow

into perfectly ordinary women
building and rebuilding

our lives. Odysseys the reading
world will never see.

We sail our ships
quietly, rough seas, roughage. Late June,

we toast over iced tea in my kitchen.
Dance to Bell Biv DeVoe

till we're cycling up Main Street to grab
falafel & Chardonnay.

Seven years ago, that blackened August,
you paid my grocery bills—that year

we grew savvy quick re
people with pockets

full of poems, full of poses.
Is there a man anywhere

on the godforsaken planet good enough
for you? It's a question worth asking.

There is hardly a thing
stronger than a woman who

sits on her porch drinking her own
hibiscus tea and eating the beets she grew

from her dirt. Who has rebuilt herself among
others, from scratch. Not in the whole vast project.

Poem for My Father

You, not long gone.
Spring's here.

My body finds its slow
way outside into
the light.

I run around the park.
Breathing.
I can do that.

Running home,
mind opens.
World opens.

This morning's sunlight
falls through the slats of the fence.

Petals fall off the rhodo
into small piles underneath:
half-moon tissue.

I run past the lilac bush
breathe in its small
mercies.

The cherry blossoms
that rang out
a month ago
announcing themselves
quiet as pink elephants
fade and fall.

Bereft, the world holds us
in its tendernesses:
a warm shawl of sunlight
the smell of cherry blossoms
after a long winter
without enough
touch.

Shark Poem

I like you in the way that I like to sit beneath bridges
and watch boats cross the water.

Sometimes I like to think about being
beneath a boat as it vees the water

until it's a wake—O the glorious ripples!
I like you in the way that I like mussels

cooked in curry and french fries
with malt vinegar on them

and a glass of Pinot Blanc when it's sunny
and when it's not.

Like I like watching films by Mike Leigh
because when everyone's wounds

bleed openly and you think happiness
is next, he pours in the iodine.

Sometimes I like you like I like black licorice
and chocolate mousse and any cake with hot caramel sauce

but could care less about profiteroles
or sugar cookies or St. Honoré.

I like you like I used to like to hide behind the furnace
with the dead snakes in it

and hear my heart knocking—excited
and terrified of being caught.

I think of you when I stare
out of this glass window

and wish that I lived in a glass house beneath the sea
and grew fields of lavender

and had many different kinds of buttons
and the sharpest hatpins

and many different record players
and records and movies starring Marilyn Monroe.

How perfect you are in a certain way, but
also flawed like when you prattle on

about whatever, using up all the air.
The world is full of people and here I am

at the coffee shop eating petite madeleines
and wondering about you.

You resemble (but aren't entirely like) a man
in a book who loves a woman with a fever

who was born in a basket
and sent downstream.

I've thought of you stumbling home from the Ocean Palace
at four a.m. haunted as Oedipus—Do you remember

the details?—a few days after he figured out
his incest, murder, plague and pestilence—oof!—

He plucked out his eyes
with a Phillips screwdriver.

Some mistakes choose you—
so leave your eyes alone.

We could swim out into the sea together
but the current would likely

pull us under, or we'd get hypothermia
and not be able to swim

back—a horrible way to disappear!

I think of you when I'm sitting inside
the car going through the automatic

car wash—the bristles and soap,
the rollers and steam feel to me

like a peep show—I mean, I like
to pay and trap myself inside the car!

And isn't it true that most people like to be
inside someone else's thoughts?

For a while I stood at the edge of a cliff
and then walked very slowly

home, and kept, the whole time,
my eyes wide. When you shot

flares out, I couldn't answer them
and by the time I could,

the world was washed out by rain
and I wanted to eat fried chicken,

sit in front of my fireplace
and listen to Édith Piaf.

Boats travel along the water
daily, breaking into the city

so quietly we rarely hear them—
just as we move through our interior lives,

unknown but happy for the anonymity
which is the centre of everything,

not the red boat with the bright searchlights
but the eels swirling in the water beneath.

Poem for Grief

Sometimes in the dark we
touch and I

wake dreaming
that I'm still holding your

cock in my hand. There is a kind
of love that commits to enduring—

That summer while I counted more tankers
moving into the inlet,

you moved out. I threw a party,
but grew so easily

exhausted that I left guests mingling
around the barbecue while I crawled

into my hammock under the oak.

What a hellacious season of indecision—
of disorientation—

of violent fissures, the shock
of waking up.

I say this from the position of
having paused in the hallway

to tell my body
where to go. Thing is—you

think you're ready for
anything; then it happens,

and you're not. You're really
not. Each day you wake up,

make lunches. Get two kids off
to school. Run for the bus.

What is ordinary saves us—

When I'm alone in the house
with the noise of the furnace,

and stare out the window at the leaves
that I've arranged and rearranged

into piles on the front lawn, I'm struck
by the sense this is what it is to experience

the world through a solitary consciousness.
This too is the luxury of living

so close to extinction: while an oil company occupies
Burnaby Mountain and the people

push in, lay their bodies down under
the tires of official trucks,

I find revolution in reading
to my daughter in bed.

"You can't even write a sentence," he said.
And so I write. This line,

replete with revolutionary energy,
is a gesture of love.

What we die to is an outworn way
of being in the world.

As if suspended in a dream,
we can barely see

what is in front of us, and in this chaos,
in this dismantling, we understand nothing.

"I am free," he said, "to build
the life I want and so are you."

And so I find myself among friends
believing resolutely in the random

character of the encounter
and the possibility of that

which endures. In what feels
radical. That declaration of eternity

descending into time. And the time
it takes the body to recover—

How does a person who loved another
and then made with that person

a third and then a fourth so easily
move on?

Some say flee.
Some say find another.

Meanwhile, the poet writes a poem
and feels a tender kind of potentiality.

And therein, chance is at last curbed.
The people hold ground at Burnaby Mountain.

The forecast calls for snow.

Poem for Loss

The sea was pulled out from
under me. Felt as if

I was ship

wrecked, marooned, cast
onto a peculiar

remoteness with rabbits
and plastic and so I

ran back toward the
sea furiously—

and there I found a

pony. He looked a little
bit like

a wearer of a heavy winter

coat. He did not ridicule me
He did not ask me

to wear bifocals or a blind-
fold or a dress made of PVC.

He did not wish to watch
me at the kitchen sink peeling

carrots. He did not need to show
me photographs to illustrate

his woundedness—

He was a gallant pony
with tender ears that, when I

spoke, bent
toward me.

I said: could I touch
your ears and he

let me. All of my life I've lived

without pedigree. My sack
of golden ducats is

empty

There are times in life
when the sea

is more beguiling than the

life boat. The pony—nay—
the pony's tenderness

carries me.

Poem for Solitude

The girls go off to their father's—
After two years the house

still feels like a tin box
& so me & Tikka—

our squawky Siamese

go for a walk; the neighbours stop
with their dogs to

talk to her, our cat who
acts like a dog.

At night, the hound of her yowling,
I dream up a sign

for her collar
that says *Free Dog*—

In the first months
after the separation,

pain in my back
woke me at three a.m.—most days

I felt like throwing up.
That first winter I roamed

the house in a diaphanous nightdress
channelling Miss Havisham—

Today butterflies flit in & out
of the windows

cracked open for fresh air.

For a year the front grass
grew cockeyed in dirt

& clay after the city

dug it up with a backhoe
to fix the drain tiles.

So I let the grass in the back
grow feral—

Then last month, I lifted four thousand

pounds of sod off the front lawn
with a shovel, tilled the dirt,

added new dirt, planted seed.
Dug up garden plots and planted

rows of Spanish lavender.
Blueberries, strawberries, cherry

tomatoes for the girls. The day is bright
when I hop on my bike

& ride through the streets
yellow & red everywhere—

So many people! People of property—

Or not. People of decency—
Or dentistry. People say,

"Everybody is just trying to get by."
Well, S is getting by in a house worth three million.

T is not. L rents a home. Most nights,
J parks her car at Queen E & sleeps in it.

I lock my bike & walk into
Coco et Olive distracted thinking about

all these inequities
& almost knock over

a woman with a ram head
tattooed on her breastbone.

I had been thinking
about my youngest girl who is dyslexic

& needs help learning to write.

I was also thinking about Alton Sterling
who, one evening last week,

was selling CDs outside Abdullah Muflahi's
convenience store in Baton Rouge, Louisiana,

when he was captured & shot
by two policemen because

he was a black man
who was selling CDs

outside Abdullah Muflahi's
convenience store

in Baton Rouge, Lousiana,
in 2016. You see, today

I quit drinking coffee.
I wrote about this good deed,

this great act of will, in my notebook
labelled *Positive Thoughts*.

At four p.m., after I chug
a single shot of espresso,

I walk two doors down
to Collage Collage

& buy a book of Hervé Tullet
group painting exercises for kids.

Poem for Rain

In my front yard
bright eyes of the
hibiscus bulge—man
cycles by the front porch *fast*, his
tail flying—bee buzzes too
close to my eye, but I don't
flinch—I'm enraptured by
the green of this place.
Hey everyone: it's finally
raining after a heat dome
lit a town on fire—
Esmeralda calls & yells
into the phone, "This
is so exciting!" By midday folks
are drinking in the park. One guy
sits apart from the crowd in
front of a concrete bench
on top of which he's drawing
an elaborate turquoise & black
totem. "It's beautiful," I say. Last
night, as we were walking together down
Hastings home from her work,
Rory chastised me for feeling sad
for everybody here. "Have you
thought that maybe given
the condition of their lives this
is, for any of them, the most
soothing way to live?"
From my front porch,
I watch a young man

playing basketball in the rain.
To see the gold in everything feels
easy &
yet—Why is it so
many men over yonder
elect to wear
socks with flip-flops
especially while
shepherding their pugs?
My hand is sticky with sugar.
Ah, the light, the light
comes bursting forth—ever
so sweet hibiscus blossom!—
white moth fluttering!—
all of it precious after rain.

Poem for Autumn

You came back to your life on a Saturday
by walking out into the pinkish-golden light.
The neighbourhood dogs smelled you for miles—
& came for you. Starting with a black Lab called Gus
who dove right into you—
A father pulled his boy's hand across the road.
Everyone walking on leaves—Do you hear it?
The sound of things dying & splitting open—
Is this not everything we're after? Each other.
A particular kind of sugar in the air.
The leaves on the oak trees the colour of tangerines.
Has it occurred to you that you know everything
you need to know to do the next thing that matters?
A black dog with a greying snout told me so.

Poem for Winter

Today the sky dumps
loads—the whole
city is covered—
& almost everything is closed: my
school, Micah's school, hardly
a car on the road
& nothing to do but
pirouette though the house singing
"Feeling Good" by
Nina Simone—
       so we make snow
angels in the sheets
before falling
back to sleep.
       Outside the snow falls
in fat flakes onto
streets covered in two
feet of snow—I wake
before she does, pull
my woollies on, my skate skis
out of the shed, glide
down my street waving to
Tony & Cecilia who are
snowed in with Logan & loop
the neighbourhood giggling
out loud at the miracle of snow & how
deliciously it halts the seemingly endless
flow of one darn thing after another.
       At Ontario Street I skate
up a slope & fly

down the other side watching
moms & dads & kids in snow pants
& overcoats, parkas & fleece,
bowl cuts, big noses, snub noses,
freckles, a heavy-set dad with
a snow-crusted beard tugs
his boy by toboggan—
Everyone is singing
themselves into the street—
At the corner of 37th and Ontario, kids
fire snowballs at each other, laughing
maniacally—what to do but
duck fast, squat down & dig for
more ammunition—
                             me against
the kids here & the ones
who come skulking
in bulky snow pants up
the hill from nearby
neighbourhoods while my
teenaged daughter sleeps—
                             Middle age simply arrives.
Too busy or blind
to notice lately I have to
put on my reading glasses
to see myself
in the mirror—who *is*
this lady? Last month, I stood
naked in my bathroom cupping
a breast in each hand, for
buoyancy, dear reader—
                             stared carefully at my face, saw

that even my forehead
is older. You know, as winter
rolls on & repeats the soul grows
deeper into this body—

   For a moment earlier this week—what was it now?—
what happened, exactly?—I felt
the contours of my daughters travelling
like celestial bodies further away from me—
as they should, moving,

   moving, gaining
volume & mass & speed, travelling across
the galaxies—

      I walked
to my closet, plucked from my top
shelf underneath my sweaters my secret
stash & dropped a tiny magic
mushroom into my tea. Isn't
mothering astonishing, really?

   You birth them. Stay
awake at night, so sleep
deprived you start seeing things,
& sometimes stupidly, you
stay up when you should be sleeping—

   waiting for her to howl out
just so you can pick her up
& nurse her back into a milky oblivion.

   Because, let's face it, you're bonkers
in love—I'd nurse her, skin

   on skin, & she'd hold my earlobe
& I'd hold her foot the size of a small potato

   in my hand. If I had a thing to do
out in the world at night her father would

soothe her cries by talking
about what I was wearing that day & whether or
not I put my hair up
or down.
                    And then, as if by
magic, she grew beyond my body
into her own—
                    I see it happening—
again & again, her coming into
her power, her
                    pushing back and forth, moving
            forward & back & forward
until she's out there, headlamp on,
roaming around in the wilderness that
always-with-me feeling of her body
out there—& always
in me.
                    As far
as her story goes, the one I've
spent a dozen years of my life writing,
I put my pen down—she picks
                            hers up, leaves scraps of paper
                            notes
hair elastics her sketchbook & pencil crayons
everywhere around the house. Middle of the night
I wake up to the sound of her
fumbling around in the kitchen
& so I tiptoe
            to the kitchen door
to see her lit up by
the fridge's snowy light foraging
in last night's leftovers

energy for her
odyssey so many
unknowns not yet
realized
delights
ahead

DESIRE LINES

Improvisation is very much about letting go of what you think it should be. There are only possibilities, there's no right and wrong.
—Lone Larsen

Look about you. Take hold of the things that are here. Let them talk to you.
—George Washington Carver

Song for the Long Days of July

Under the zelkova's pale shade
      flesh of my peach falls off its pit—

                    kids next door are bent over in the grass
                chatting with the ground beetles—

Bless them & their big questions,
      feelings bursting forth like sprinkler water—

      With the what-ifs of fall looming,

my mind wanders while the neighbourhood
      floats around me & the sky hangs

in a perfect sheet of light—

      In the dream that is lately with me,
                  I'm dancing with you across this
                  vast landscape

    of our living room reading
the language of your body, new

      dreams moving us forward—

To braid my girl's hair in the park,
      her head in my lap—

to touch that one

dark mole left of her hairline—

    Bees loop around the frothy
heads of our lavender—

Despite their rotting leaves, our green tomatoes
    bloom into red

pleasure—Sometimes all it takes is
    a garden.

Or, out in the woods,
    a smear of thimbleberry.

Walking up & down a mountain trail & then

        a meadow of wildflowers—

The white-petalled face of the western
    anemone says, *Well, hi there*

Tubular bloom of the shrubby penstemon
    hangs open like a hard feeling

released—When we swam naked in Slocan Lake
    our bodies glowed

All week we dropped our pants
    & peed on trees—

ambled back into the wildernesses
of our childhoods among neighbours

talking to the hoary marmot
& tinkering creek—

That last night we paddled quietly,
dipped our oars in & out of the water—

Poem for May 2020

The plane heard me
& we blued the roof

on a Sunday afternoon
you sourdoughing

the new bok choy singing to
the boys next door

playing ball—

The smell of lavender
summons my mother

the sound of her bathwater—
water that felt as if it was

falling—it *was* falling—
all of a sudden you

are beside me it's May
your feet appear

Are we ever going to stop
harvesting arugula?

It's peaceful, you know—
so many plants growing

me on the deck outside
writing in a trance

you in the kitchen making
bread with walnuts in it

The sound of a neighbour's
jig saw four doors down

amid melting ice caps & meteors & viral
overloads, we keep making

love, isn't that
something?

So many wavelets
between us

Do you hear that
tinkling sound? Shoot, I must've

left the hose on—
Nevertheless

we dance in the kitchen
passing parsley mouth to mouth

Last night I dreamt
I slept beside an earl

fussed with his lapels
& tassels—you kissed

a duchess. We woke up
on a Sunday

talking about this very serious
business—

What happened was
we walked into the woods

What happened was
a mood I felt

a tenderness I
thought possible

Of course I'm
tired—let's go

walking into the woods
together—let's sit by

the asters & drink
black tea with a swig of milk

Gosling & gosling & gosling
& goose

I've been meaning to tell you,
I bake pies with my reveries inside them

You're the sound of
the only plane in the sky

for miles listen to the neighbour
going bonkers with his pressure

washer the neighbours—so aloof!—
are finally talking to each other

Which reminds me, I have to phone
my mother

                    Mom,
what are we doing here?

We could pack it all in
& buy a camper van

do some noodling—Will you
walk with me into the

woods for a while?
If we're quiet,

rivulet, will you
wave? Bring me your

flying saucer, love,
your lozenges

We lay down in a
meadow together

spoon the night sky—

While Walking Inside the Langara Golf Course Dreaming About Dr. Bonnie Henry, April 21, 2020

This morning I woke up, did
yoga, put eggs in the freezer.
How long will we go on not
touching each other? I miss
my mother. I miss nuzzling my closest friends,
walking in the city among others
taking in gardens & graffiti without
worrying about droplets—sitting beside
strangers in public parks. Grocery shopping
without panic. Living room dance parties
that go on into the wee hours—
Singing together. Feasts.
Every single bullshit
problem I had back in February.
I want to be among
people at Prado & the Fox Cabaret. I want
to go square dancing
at the Wise Hall, stand in Clark Park hula
hooping with hoops wrapped in shiny ribbons
that spin our bodies into
iridescent fish—I want
colleagues again, even the ones who
spring their dumb-ass questions
just as the meeting is wrapping up—
Yesterday we pulled a nearly burned
sourdough from the oven & ate
the whole thing. I counted eleven new
blossoms on the star magnolia. Note:
the lettuce leaves have doubled in size.

The sage blooms are a purple so bright they blink.
How easy, this cataloguing of beauty—
If this pandemic *is* a portal, what will we
do? I'll trade you
my eleven thousand lawn mowers, three unicorn banks,
my million Mercedes Benzes with rooftop dance
party platform for guaranteed income for all.
Will you greet me, dear stranger?
How about you with your earbuds & your lacquered
lashes? Dear elderly lady who walks
with a cane & whose eyes say "Bugger off," dear
adult in bloom your body slumped over in a benzo high
& frozen—what if every night we
set up a table outside on our
boulevards or porches & set it with plates, cutlery, a pot
of hot curry? What if every alley had a community
fridge so whoever is hungry could
stop by & stock up? Thank the gods we
bought a machine to make espresso at home before
the coffee shops closed. We sit here
breakfast, lunch & dinner staring
into each other's eyebrows, cozy &
craving to be among.
     Awake ye, please
come to our house—come
running—

Dinner Party

We sat at a table in the backyard
under lanterns and twinkling lights.

The older kids talked about going off to college,
about the feeling of wanting

to be—above all—free. "Who exactly
owns Vancouver," C asked, "the people

or the money?" Q drew us a picture
with arrows to show us

how it's broken down into chunks & laundered—

We talked about banks, ailing
parents, menopause

That feeling, you know—being together,
the drunken glitches—laughter

peeling us all slightly more open

until stories bloomed from
everyone's mouths. Even the kids

were in on it. Ah, that feeling
in you is in me too—

We ate BBQ. Drank too many
glasses of wine. Later, we heard

the sky popping open—

Someone said, "Jeezus that sounds like gun shots—"
Someone else suggested it was the Celebration of Light

We talked about fascism, ours,
theirs, but also about hope as that feathered thing

that moves us toward
each other—

We hatched a plan among
mothers to go

microdose some LSD.
When the feeling of sleep

hit, the twinkling lights carried
me by bicycle across the city

across the cool air
across all the imperfect

details of my life—

Illuminations

We started coatless up the old
logging road to Deeks Lake not much
more sound than our footfalls,
found a waterless pond filled
with sand & silvery trunks & walked on
softly up into the woods past
waxy rows of salal & goldenrod.

Wherever they could, the girls spotted
sun on wood & rested awhile inside
the smell of balsam & fir—

We saw scars in the trunks photographed
weird fungus fit the tips of our fingers
with salmonberries felt
the smoke from the summer's
abominable fires ghosting us finally.
We walked up into the switchbacks covered
in pine needles   rocks   endless roots exposed
polished by boot soles—

When the trail grew steeper and greener
I listened for water tinkling over rocks like glass
prayer beads rattling up against each other
& later   the closer we walked to the top
            the more the water gathered
its loose sounds into a roar & erupted down the rocks—

When we saw the bewildering
green Deeks Lake finally—
alpine lake surrounded by rocks
surrounded by woods surrounded by water—
we put our packs down
& waded into water
so cold it was painful.

I dove in & under & ambled back up
onto a rock where I sat for
elongated minutes in the quiet
lake glimmering in the gold-
green August light. Somehow we
swam, ate, dried off & dressed again.

On their way out of the mountain lake
the two girls turned their shirts up into baskets
& filled them with wild blueberries
they plucked from the bushes.

For a moment I watched the other girl not mine
standing on the path in the rutilant light her hair
almost aflame her hands inside
a ball of light. One hand holding her shirt
the other inspecting a single berry and then bringing it
to her mouth—

Later that evening she told me quietly
about the first blood she found on her underwear
dark miracle of beginnings & fire,
the world blooming inside her—

These Seasons We Wander

Outside the door out
there in the woods
buttercups appear
the colour of childhood.

A child of five by the creek feeling
the rhythm of the creek water
against her yellow head.

Tell me how it feels
to be(long) lost in the woods—

     *

Back then, our crabapples
our tree forts,
our peanut butter & jelly
sandwiches & our Jos Louis—what
we snuck into the trees with us.

Now, we set out with our Blundstones.
Our light sabers.
Our reach-ins.
Our packets of vitamin C.

     *

There is so much to know
about uncertainty
as a wayfinder—

So many more possibilities.

*

Here in the woods
is the beginning.
Is the ending.

The cedars of the Cupressaceae family
are turning orange.

O ever-weakening roots—
Ours, too.

*

What good does this beauty do us
if the cedars are dying?

*

Back home in the garden
the coreopsis hangs out in me—
Butterflies roam   Home
is a garden of wildflowers
filled with poppies whose
dried seed pods
I squash with my fingers
Whose seeds the winds & I scatter
by hand—

*

My ear tuned to you,
we commingle
on the hardwood—

the rustling the yowling
out the windows—

*

Fall comes. The local weather
more mercurial than ever,
O heat dome
O bomb cyclone
Behold this
new lexicon
we're all learning—

Nevertheless
I stand inside the maple's yellow
skirt, leaves that fall
like dancers
to the ground
that stick out
like stars. Yellow
ravaged interiors,
crimson edges.

Practice

Now the rain has let up and the pies are in.

Now the streets are dark and slick. I hear Tony next door slamming
    his car door after a long day working electrical.

Now the cat is licking her paw.

Now I sit here in the light without my brother who has left to go back
    up the mountain, but I feel traces of him in me.

Now I sip lemon tea.

Now I'm covered in an afghan.

Now I'm trying to connect with the weather inside me.

Now my eyes are older.

Acoustic Showing

September night, cool air.
Sound of a distant siren floats in.
Cars emerge like fricatives
& frig off to somewhere else—
Never been a boy but oh boy
am buoyed by the thought of a cock
like a beautifully wrought ampersand.
Finally, the rain pounds down,
a cold rain, & my body wants wool,
wants sleep in flannel sheets.
Close my eyes and think of one of two
big-bodied Williams while droplets
caught by magnolia leaves tremble
& fall. Coyotes cry out from the golf course—
sounds like they are seriously getting it on!
I do this, I do that, while the Fraser River
water moves along—the rhythm of salmon
sniffing out the water for clues to get back home.
So much has happened here—
all the tugboats and brokering.
All the men with their hooks in big trees.
It's weird work this being here together
on this earth. Bless the vegans. Bless
the bridge builders. Bless the souls
among us who, like me, are as lonely as skunk cabbage.
I want an electrical storm, I want
a meteor shower, I want
the whole fucking Milky Way
to show up like swirling silver
ribbons in the sky. I want a meatier

hour than this. A kind of thickening.
To feel a quiet cueing.
To be, above all, as curious as
as words. As slippery as water—
To hold the purslane in my dirty hands,
to tug its lace gently from the earth & hold it
up & snip each tiny leaf for eating.
To be as beautiful as crickets bleating
into the pitch-black night—
As loving as the cedars sounding, tending, tendering,
dying & standing by.

Poem for Water

In my dream, I was travelling in Tucson
& watching on a TV screen two planes flying into a building,
a tall, wide & many-dark-windowed Vancouver building—
indistinguishable building with very
important business going on inside.
Sent a flurry of texts but couldn't reach either
one of my girls whose real lives are going on,
more or less, without me. Just this morning
they fell off the couch laughing when I called Cardi B
Carby D. The comedy of aging—
Am thinking this morning about Rita who was arrested yesterday
while blocking traffic to the Kinder Morgan
site on Burnaby Mountain. I went to bed with the picture
of her sitting with her legs crossed on the pavement,
her long black hair shoulders
wrapped in a wool blanket & cedar smoke,
the elders around her singing
the Tsleil-Waututh water song for
protection—even when the police read her
her rights she kept quietly
singing. When Athena disguised herself
as Mentes to help Telemachus, she told him,
"Be brave and win yourself a lasting name,"
& then changed herself into a bird & flew into
the sky. The epic story of a man whose grand adventure
was simply to go back home. All these millennia water flows—
Anthropocene brings gyres of plastic, dead fish & coral,
a seabed of bitumen & toxic spew: whether we'll see
deeply what is going on right in front of us
might be the most formidable epic of all. The sign

outside this café window says, *Ermagerd!!! A garage sale!*
Saturday, August 25 at Ontario and 20th.
So much commerce to cover. So many things
to savour for a while & sell. So much of life
asking us to move through it like water, not holding
too hard nor too fast to too much.

Songs from the Bottle-Dash Stucco

Though the girls aren't with us this week
I feel their phantom bodies
beside me. You look almost
dead when you sleep—you and the curved
tips of your overgrown toenails,
two honking pork steaks for feet—
I might nest in your chest mañana,
sniff you out by the smell of your salt—
For now, I'm just trying to hear
the noise the neighbours make
kicking a soccer ball around
against the sound of you snoring in your dreams—
So much history you've missed—
Flashback: Micah is six and she's chasing butterflies—
It might help to read the annals on this house:
champion horse racer lived here.
Two-timing winner of the Langara calculus contest.
A family of dentists from Belgrade who saved up
& left for the Westside with their Siamese.
Twenty years ago a man tried to grab
a woman by the throat by this front door
but she ducked that goose—
planted rows of lavender and bright-eyed peonies
that come up singing every spring.

Poem for Maggie

Walking out along this icy path heading
down from Sleeping Buffalo Mountain

with Maggie—we're soaked in big mountain
light—I wonder what my new

instrument will be   this light   these legs walking me
to new places

away from what doesn't matter so much
away from the old stories that emerge

like big boulders blocking the river
boulders that stop things up—What is it?

Walking to stay open against
the fear of not having enough

the fear of yet another loss—
the desire to protect my girls

All our lives we're moving
boulders so the water flows

on—It's springtime on Sleeping

Buffalo; along the railway, the
grizzly they call the Boss meanders

for grain. *When the Boss emerges some folks
panic*, the elder says, *but bears*

*teach us how to survive. If
they're good, we're good.*

They're here with us, Maggie,
in the woods.

Poem for Experience

The castle walk is long.
Outside, peach trees.
Sparrows. A world sprung up.
Everything green is prone—
Inside, this window
that I've lived a life looking out of—
Deliberations. Obsessions. Spells
that make magic plus
a lesser magic. *Excess*
of sorrow laughs, excess
of joy weeps. About a decade
in, I wrote, *Joy*
finds a boat
and goes out
onto the ocean. Beckons
a pony &
a boy. From inside
these walls, I divined
a man-boy of about eighteen
who wears a straw hat,
who meanders barefoot,
who carries a big-mouthed cymbal
to clatter the lurking beasts,
to buoy me. He knows
the labyrinthine caves
of this place
like his mother tongue.
Finally, a gentle man
who'll hold his shoulder
to the wheel for me.

O my lovely peach tree,
summon all your silver-haired angels,
your merry sparrows,
we've got satchels packed, we're
heading in—

Walking Up and Down Sleeping Buffalo Mountain

In a blizzard
        wearing borrowed
crampons I walk up
        Sleeping Buffalo
where for ten thousand years
        the Stoney Nakoda & the Tsuut'ina
gathered medicines among the spruce
        & limber pines.
When the firs open up, I look out
        at a town below built
around a castle and a bejewelled cave
        where the Stoney built their ke'kuli,
        four-thousand-year-old
pit houses that were found
        & filled up
for eighteen holes of "breathtaking views."
        We're here
in Banff at a writers' retreat studying
        the art of walking. Rilke,
who gave his first-born
        to his wife's parents
to raise, wrote in his famous letters
        about his vast inner solitude—
the chance to walk, he said, is
        a chance to walk inside yourself
for hours—
        but I miss
the soft faces of my girls,
        their teenage banter and laughter, even
the flat affect of their faces

after being woken up.
At the summit I find
	a fine fog settling in, stop
to watch two whiskyjacks poking
	around in the treetops—walk
down the icy paths of Sleeping Buffalo,
	walking not out of fidelity
to solitude but for the pleasure
	of moving forward. I say to
myself over and over,
	You make your way
home by going farther—

Notes on the Poems

"Reveries of a Walker Walking Among Others" is a riff on Jean-Jacques Rousseau's *Reveries of a Solitary Walker*. This poem was written for my late father, John Jerome, whose spirit is alive among the cedars. "When you died it was like a whole library burned down" comes from an elegiac song called "World Without End" that Laurie Anderson wrote for her father; it's from her album *Bright Red*.

In the poem "Atmosphere," the first direct quotation comes from Lee Maracle's formidable, heartbreaking essay, "Goodbye Snauq." In the second quotation, BC Attorney General W.J. Bowser tells the Squamish living at the Kitsilano reserve (Snauq), "There you are. Here is your cheque with your name on it for $11,250. Take it. If you do not, you will never get a cent for your reserve." This quotation is cited in Jean Barman's essay "Erasing Indigenous Indigeneity in Vancouver" (BC *Studies*, no. 155, Autumn 2007). The quotation's original source is a *Province* article, "Red Men Took Cash from Mr. Bowser This Morning," published on April 9, 1913.

The Squamish welcome pole, a K'aya'chtn pole, that appears in "Atmosphere" was made by master carver Darren Yelton. It is waiting for you, arms outstretched, at the start of the old CPR line by Burrard Street Bridge, between Vanier Park and Granville Island. This k'aya'chtn was created from a five-hundred-year-old red cedar tree from the Elaho Valley.

The quotation about Changsha, Zen Master Jingcen, that appears in "Atmosphere" comes from Dogen Zenji's "Valley Sounds, Mountain Colors" (*Treasury of the True Dharma Eye*, eds. Kazuaki Tanahashi and Peter Levitt).

"The Messenger" was inspired by a long walk in Stanley Park with Tom Green, followed by the collaborative creation of a *cadavre exquis* poem made spontaneously over breakfast at the Greenhorn Cafe on January 24, 2020.

"Often I'm Permitted to Return to These Cedars" is a title reminiscent of Robert Duncan's famous poem "Often I Am Permitted to Return to a Meadow."

In "Poem for Grief," the first couplet comes from the poem "You" by Frank Stanford, the eleventh from "only the crossing counts" by C.D. Wright. The lines "what is in front of us, and in this chaos,/ in this dismantling, we understand nothing" are abridged from a sentence in Jean-Jacques Rousseau's first walk in *Reveries of a Solitary Walker*: "I have been in this strange situation for fifteen years or more, and it still seems as if I must be dreaming. I still imagine that I must be suffering from indigestion, that I must be sleeping badly, and that I am going to wake up and find myself relieved of my pain and back among my friends again. Yes, it must be, I must without realizing it have made the leap from being awake to being asleep, or rather from being alive to being dead. Wrenched somehow how out of the normal order of things, I have been thrown into an incomprehensible chaos in which I can make out nothing at all, and the more I think about my current situation, the less I understand where I am." The lines "that declaration of eternity/ descending into time" are what Stéphane Mallarmé said about poetry. Finally, the third from the last line of the poem, "And therein, chance is at last curbed," comes from Alain Badiou's *In Praise of Love*.

The last lines of the poem "While Walking Inside the Langara Golf Course Dreaming About Dr. Bonnie Henry, April 21, 2020" come from the first two lines of a poem by C.D. Wright called "Girl Friend Poem #2" from the collection *Steal Away: Selected and New Poems*.

"Poem for Experience" came from a workshop curated by poet Deb Woodard in which she gave me an image and the italicized lines from William Blake's "Proverbs of Hell" in his book *The Marriage of Heaven and Hell.*

The last line of "Walking Up and Down Sleeping Buffalo Mountain" comes from a line from "Wanderer's Nightsong II" by Johann Wolfgang von Goethe.

Acknowledgements

Thank you to the Musqueam, Squamish and Tsleil-Waututh peoples for the land we get to walk on every day, land this book, this life, is indebted to.

So much thanks to my communities of family, friends, neighbours and colleagues for their support: Laura Repas, Stephanie Keon, Elena Johnson, Heidi Ravenel, Laura Moss, Mandy Catron, Naava Smolash, TC Tolbert, Sommer Browning, Treena Chambers, Samir Gandesha, Maggie Ziegler, Mary Schendlinger, Anakana Schofield, Heather Low, Mark Grenon, Ljiljana Bukovic and Goran Basaric. Thanks to new friends Keiron Simons and Maryam Abasi, Oriana Graber, Julie Shipman, Kim Marshall, Adrian Ruigrok, Steve McAdam, Andrea Jung, Erik Olafson and sweet Sasha for many cherished get-togethers and laughs.

Thank you to the Canada Council for the Arts and the BC Arts Council for grants that made the writing of this book possible. Thanks to my students at UBC, and my English department colleagues at UBC, as well as new colleagues and students at Gladstone Secondary. I'm so grateful to be spending the second half of my life among teenagers who are also my teachers. Thanks to Alicia Ostroff, Kristin Green and Corin Browne for our many walks and talks on Friday afternoons. Thanks to other friends in teaching for helping me take the dive from university to high school teaching: Lusheen Beaumont, Brittney Mallett, Sara Zacharia, Cosette Francis, Tanya Zambrano, Dustin Keller, Ryan Peters, Greg Sutherland, Ken Ipe and Penny Turpin, Nancy Serra-Campos and Lawrence Jakoy.

Raoul Fernandes was both receiver and transmitter on every single page of this manuscript. So too was Silas White, dear editor and publisher. My thanks to him and to everyone else at Nightwood for making this book.

Thanks to my family: my mother Colleen Kerr, my brothers Paddy and Brendan, my sisters-in-law Kate Erwin and Amanda Webb, my nephews Lukas and Koen, and the Green family, especially Les Green, Marion Green, Jenny Green and Steve Brazeau for their love and support. Thanks most of all to my daughters, Rory and Micah, and my partner in life, Tom Green, for looking up at houses on jack posts and seeing boats in the sky.

PHOTO CREDIT: ERIN FLEGG

About the Author

Gillian Jerome is a mother, writer, teacher who lives on the unceded land of the xʷməθkʷəy̓əm (Musqueam), Sḵwx̱wú7mesh (Squamish) and Selílwitulh (Tsleil-Waututh) Nations, land and water she is grateful for and responsible to. Her first book of poems, *Red Nest* (Nightwood Editions, 2009), was nominated for the Dorothy Livesay Poetry Prize and won the 2010 ReLit Award for Poetry. She co-edited an oral history project, *Hope in Shadows: Stories and Photographs from Vancouver's Downtown Eastside* (Arsenal Pulp Press, 2008), which won the 2008 City of Vancouver Book Award.